IMAGES
of America

WARE

THE MANOUR OF PEACE

This building, on the corner of Bank and Main Streets, began as the Hampshire Manufacturers Bank in 1825. When state banks ended in 1864, it then became the Ware National Bank. Today, Ware National Bank notes can still be found in collections. The young elm trees seen in this picture were planted by William S. Hyde before the turn of the century. Like the many elms that once graced the Main Street, they fell victim to Dutch Elm disease. Note that the picture on the box to the left of the wagon is an advertisement for the newfangled water closet, or flush toilet.

IMAGES
of America

WARE
THE MANOUR OF PEACE

Warren Bacon and Claudia Chicklas

ARCADIA

First published 1996
Copyright © Warren Bacon and Claudia Chicklas, 1996

ISBN 0-7524-0453-9
Published by Arcadia Publishing,
an imprint of the Chalford Publishing Corporation
One Washington Center, Dover, New Hampshire 03820
Printed in Great Britain

Library of Congress Cataloging-in-Publication Data applied for

Contents

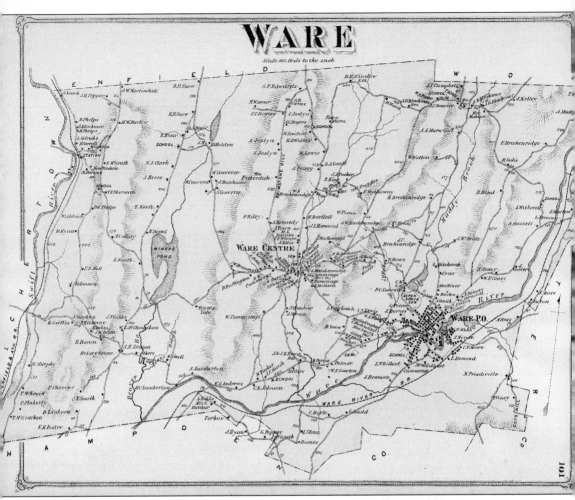

A map of Ware Center and the Ware Post Office in 1873.

Introduction

The Ware River Precinct, which came into existence in 1742, was originally included in land known as the Elbow Tract, a part of Hampshire County. When a dispute arose between the colonies of Connecticut and Massachusetts over the boundary between the two, the matter was settled by a compromise which allowed Massachusetts to retain the border towns in dispute, while compensating Connecticut by giving her an equal amount of undeveloped territory in Massachusetts. This area was known as the "Equivalent Lands" and Connecticut was expected to realize financial reimbursement from the sale of this land, which was purchased by a company of proprietors. The purchase price of £683 was voted to Yale College. Among the proprietors was John Read, a minister and lawyer, who thus became owner of approximately 11,000 acres of land, the larger part of the territory of Ware.

Mr. Read planned to develop this land in the model of an English manor, and gave it the name "The Manour of Peace," possibly to entice people to settle here. He leased out the land rather than offering it for sale, although he did donate 200 acres upon which to establish a church and glebe, or parsonage. The first lease on record was to Henry Dwight in 1726. The precinct, or parish, that was established in 1742 gave inhabitants independence only in their religious affairs, but in 1761 Ware was incorporated as a district without representation in the General Court. When the General Court convened at the beginning of the Revolution in 1775, it granted Ware full town privileges. The early town developed in the area of the Flat Brook, where the Ware Centre Meeting House still stands.

In the early 1800s, the core population of Ware shifted from Ware Centre to Ware Factory Village on the Ware River, the present business and administrative center of town. The main highways of the town, some laid out 8 or 10 rods wide, saw much traffic, including four or six-horse coaches that carried both passengers and freight. The Monson Turnpike, running from Athol to Monson, was authorized to collect tolls of 25¢ for a "chariot" drawn by two horses; 5¢ for every man and horse; and 3¢ a dozen for sheep and swine. In 1821, Thomas Denny and Alpheus Demond bought 400 acres along the Ware River and built a new dam to take advantage of the available water power. The Ware Manufacturing Company was incorporated and it erected a woolen mill on the south side of the river in 1823. The next year they built a larger mill up river, using power from the upper falls. By 1839, the Otis Company was organized and built a large brick mill and a stone mill on the site.

The growth of the mills had a dramatic effect on the population of the town, as the rapidly increasing need for workers attracted people first from outlying farms, followed by immigrants from England, Ireland, Canada, and Poland. The following notes help to illustrate the impact of the growing Otis Company on the town during the nineteenth century. Valuation of the company's property in 1842 was $43,793, while valuation in 1910 had reached $1,120,050. In 1840, there were 211 people on the Otis Company's payroll; by 1911 this number had grown to 1,875. Production in 1840 was 744,465 yards, while by 1910, the company boasted 16,000,000 yards of cloth and 360,000 dozens underwear. As an interesting aside, records show that 3,000 gallons of whale oil were used between 1849 and 1850 to light the mills. In addition to textiles, Ware industries also produced straw goods, boots, and shoes, and a number of small businesses grew along the Main Street in response to the markets created by the expanding population of mill employees.

When the Great Depression of the 1930s struck the country, and textile manufacturing in particular, Ware was dealt a near fatal blow. However, her citizens were able to work together and pull the town through the crisis. The textile mills are no longer the major employers, but the mill complex still exists, harboring an interesting collection of growing businesses, including antiques, art, retail outlets, and a restaurant within its historic walls.

Many scenes of the evolution of the town and the mills from the 1880s to the 1960s come from the collection of the Ware Historical Society, located at 11 Church Street in the Senior Center in Ware. We dedicate this book to the founding members of our historical society, and particularly to Bill Towlson, our first president, whose vision made the society's collection possible.

One
Main Street and
Nenameseck Square

One of a five-picture set taken by Charles Eddy in 1885 titled "A Bird's Eye View of Ware." Since aerial photographs were not possible at that time, Mr. Eddy climbed into the town hall tower to make the exposures. The original town hall was erected here in 1846 at a cost of $4,500. A fire in November 1867 consumed the building, along with the Unitarian church next door and a house in the rear. Its replacement, from which these photographs were taken, was built between 1885 and 1886. The land was far more cleared than it is today and the surrounding hills had been cut over frequently, like much of rural Massachusetts, leaving a meager growth of young trees rather than mature forest. This view looks southeast over the mills and a portion of Water Street (now Pulaski Street).

A view of the town looking north from the town hall. Snow's Pond and the cemetery are at the upper left.

A view of West Main Street from the town hall tower. George Eddy's boot factory and sand banks can be seen on the extreme right.

Saint William's Catholic Church and Cemetery (in the upper left), looking southwest from the town hall.

Main Street, looking east from the town hall. The Unitarian church spire is in the foreground. Starting on the far left, readers can see the Congregational, French Catholic, and Methodist church spires.

Main Street. One auto parked here has a 1933 registration, but some cars look to be an earlier model year.

Main Street's south side on a Saturday afternoon in 1933. All the parking spaces have been taken by shoppers.

Waiting to get into the fire sale at the Trench Block in October 1907. This location later housed the J.J. Newberry's store.

The F.W. Woolworth store shortly after World War I. The store closed in 1961.

The Hampshire House before the turn of the century. It has been said that William Howard Taft spoke from the portico on a visit to Ware.

The Hampshire House, in the early 1900s. By this time, Coca Cola was becoming a popular drink.

The Ware Town Hall about 1910, when it was also called the Opera House. Although built between 1885 and 1886, the clock and Westminster chimes were added in 1901, a gift of the Storrs family. Local talent as well as vaudeville acts and stock companies played on this building's stage. The structure suffered a fire in January 1935, suffering damage estimated at $60,000. The building reopened in March 1935, was rebuilt at a cost of $105,000, and remains in use today. The street sign at the corner gives the distances to Ware Center, West Ware, and Enfield, the latter of which was taken by the M.D.C. in the 1930s to make the Quabbin Reservoir.

February 10, 1926. When this image was taken, the town had just come through a bad winter storm. The Ware Trust Company had replaced the old National Bank by this time.

Another view from the storm of February 1926. The snow was loaded onto trucks by men with shovels.

A view of the Casino Theater, which was moved here from Parker Street in 1913, and the Mansion House. Early vaudeville acts played at the Casino.

The express carts of John F. O'Connor. These wagons were kept busy hauling freight from the railroad and moving local loads.

A clerk stands in front of the old A&P store on a summer morning in 1939. This Main Street store served customers from Ware and all nearby towns.

Beautiful Nenameseck Square before the Grey Block fire. The Ware Cooperative Bank parking lot now occupies the space where the brick building stood.

A winter scene of the old bank and Bank Street. This lovely view brings us back to the time of gas lights and sleighs.

The Young Men's Library Association building dressed up in patriotic bunting for Ware's 150th anniversary celebration in 1911.

Lower North Street showing the side of the Storrs Block, Lance Hotel, and the new post office in the late 1930s.

The 1887 Mansion House, one of Ware's grand old buildings. It was destroyed by fire in October 1975.

A midday view of the north side of Main Street between Bank and North Streets.

The south side of Main Street from lower North Street, without the trees which line the street today.

The Kaplan Block. This group of businesses was severely damaged by fire in 1927, but the block was rebuilt shortly thereafter.

A rare old picture from the 1800s, featuring a clock and a boot. Hitching posts line Main Street, somewhat like the parking meters we had a few years ago. It didn't cost anything to park back then, but an occasional deposit was left anyway.

Two
Business and Industry

The Otis Company's counting house, 1884. There were saw and gristmills at the Ware River falls soon after 1729, and by 1830 an iron furnace, machine shop, and cotton and woolen mills were located there. Manufacturing on a significant scale at this site dates from the 1830s and '40s when a five-story brick mill and a stone mill were erected. The Otis Company was organized in 1839 with 211 employees, whose monthly production was 62,000 yards of material. By the 1880s, the company employed about 1,350 people and produced yard goods, underwear, and stockings. The counting house is pictured here with the No. 3 mill in the background. This is said to be the first complete knitting mill in the world; manufacturing from baled stock to the finished garment.

The Charles A. Stevens Company mill building, originally built in 1825. This structure was expanded in 1851 by adding another story and an addition that augmented its length by 70 feet. At the time of this 1884 photograph there were 175 employees who produced opera flannels and dress goods.

The George H. Gilbert Company's office on South Street in 1884. Incorporated in 1857, this business manufactured woolens and worsteds for men's wear.

The George H. Gilbert mills, 1884. The mill property was purchased in 1841 by a partnership, Gilbert and Stevens, which dissolved in 1851. George Gilbert retained the operation south of the river.

The No. 3 mill, 1886. The original building on this site was the Hampshire Co. machine shop where, it is said, Sam Colt made his first gun—which exploded when fired.

The site of the old boiler house in the mill complex, 1887.

The J.T. Wood Company boot factory in 1913. This company was established in 1891 and was originally located on Mechanic Street.

A tractor in use by the Ware Woolen company in the 1920s.

The first automatic loom for the weaving of flannel at Ware Woolen, 1927.

An aerial view of the mill yard in 1939. The South Street bridge, at lower left, had been rebuilt after the 1938 flood. The mills suffered reverses in the Depression years and the Otis Company, Ware's largest employer for nearly a hundred years, decided to liquidate in 1937. Townspeople rallied behind a plan to raise funds to purchase the mills. This action gained national attention and Ware became known as "The Town That Can't Be Licked," a phrase coined by Police Chief Bartholomew W. Buckley. As a result, The Ware Industries, Incorporated was organized in November 1937.

The Ware Woolen Mill viewed from across the river in the 1930s.

The Hampshire Woolen Mill on East Street in the 1930s.

Office staff of the Ware Valley Mfg. Co., makers of Otis Underwear, *c.* 1930.

Ware Industries officers and workers, seated by the Stone Mill, 1930s.

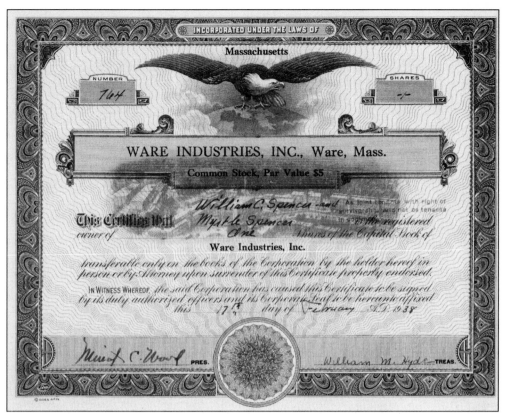

Ware Industries common stock share, 1938. Only one dividend was ever paid on this common stock.

The Ware Gas Light Company plant and storage tank. Originally begun as a collateral operation of the Otis Company, the Gas Company was sold in 1930 to the American Commonwealth Power Company.

An early picture taken by O.O. Cross, a merchant tailor and photographer.

A fine winter occupation—cutting ice on Snow's Pond in the 1920s.

Lane's Grocery, with a large load of Lane's Best Flour, *c.* 1890.

The hardware department of Augustin Terrien's store, established 1887. Augustin also sold furniture, carpets, staple groceries, fresh fish, and other items for the thrifty housewife.

Dr. Miner's Drug Store, advertising cures for corns and many other ailments, *c.* 1890.

The delivery of a boiler, drawn by four oxen and two mules, *c.* 1890s.

A piece of heavy equipment, drawn by a team of horses, featuring a sign that reads "George C. Wesson, Contractor." Workers and a company official are in the foreground.

The Ware River News office in the 1890s. First published in 1887, it continues as a weekly paper today.

The Hastings Motor Company shortly after World War II. Hastings combined auto service and appliance sales and service.

Bousquet's service station on West Street in the days before self-serve.

The Endicott-Johnson Shoe store. Endicott-Johnson returned to its location in the Hitchcock block after the fire in 1959.

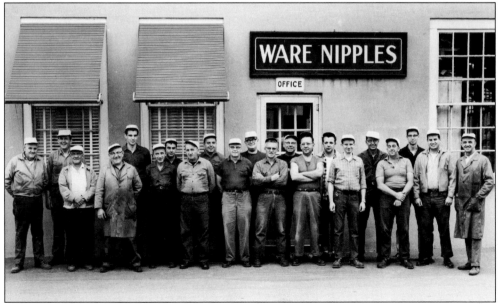

The Ware Nipples plant in 1967. This company, which fabricates pipe, was established in 1917 by Donald W. Howe, who took over a bankrupt shed and built it into a successful business.

A group of Ware businessmen in the 1930s.

The Ware Telephone Company building on Bank Street, erected in 1939.

Three
Streets, Homes, and Scenic Views

The Bijou Theater. Located on the second floor of the Kaplan Block, this was one of four picture houses in Ware in 1918. The others were the Casino, the town hall, and the Durrell Theater. Earlier, in a transition from vaudeville to films, the Bijou advertised *The Prisoner of Zenda* in "four big reels" and named the star, James K. Hackett. And it was the Bijou that featured the famous serial, *The Perils of Pauline*, which kept people hanging from week to week as Pauline went from crisis to crisis.

The Lafayette Elm. It was said that in 1894 Lafayette rested under this tree, which was said to be 320 years old when it blew over in a 1923 storm.

The original East Street Bridge, built in 1848. This structure was washed out in the flood of 1869, was rebuilt, and was washed out once again in 1938.

Ware photographer Charles W. Eddy's house on Eddy Court in 1882.

The Ware Hotel at Main and North Streets. Also known as the Delevan House, this establishment replaced the Phelps Hotel, which burned in 1864.

The Wesson homestead on North Street, home of George Wesson, a trucker and superintendent of roads.

The old Glebe House in Ware Center, said to be the oldest house in Ware.

Spring Street, as viewed from High Street. This photograph was taken when streets and sidewalks were not paved and homes were lighted with kerosene lamps.

The house located just below the old French church on Bank Street, now the site of the telephone building.

A fine old home on Union Street. The house still looks much the same, but the trees have grown older and are much larger.

Lower West Street past Robbins Road in the days when the road surface was dirt and the trolley tracks ran alongside.

Looking toward Main Street from West Street. The school is to the left in the foreground.

The Narrows in Grenville Park, where the Hadley Path crossed the Ware River in colonial times.

The covered bridge, probably built in 1886, that connects Ware and Gilbertville. The white line in the middle of the bridge marked the boundary line between towns.

The clubhouse at Beaver Lake in 1893, home of the Ware Rod and Gun Club.

The dam which held back the water of Beaver Brook forming Beaver Lake in 1893.

The Beaver Lake Clubhouse bowling alley, complete with hanging kerosene lamps, also in 1893.

The former Ware Post Office, due to be renovated for use as the new police station in the near future.

St. Mary's Rectory. This building was purchased from the Otis Company. Previously it was the residence of C.E. Blood.

Four
Transportation

Oxen resting on Main Street. These animals' peaceful and patient natures made them a good choice for drawing heavy wagons through the dust and mud of unpaved thoroughfares. Here, they stop in front of the Old Tavern House as they wait for their next load. In this pre-1895 photograph, the office of John Yale, M.D., who began practicing in Ware in 1846, is visible in the left rear. The Hitchcock Block, on the site of the old tavern, later housed the Endicott-Johnson Shoe store and the Acropolis Pizza.

The Ware Sleigh, an antique believed to have been built in 1775.

A team with a natty driver and a load in the wagon of the George Wesson company around 1900.

A wood-burning steam locomotive on the way to Barre, Massachusetts, around 1870.

The busy Union Station in Ware, around 1918. By 1932, passenger service on the Boston and Maine was discontinued.

Ladies waiting for the train, *c.* 1920.

Weigh while you wait; Union Station in the 1920s.

A horse and trolley on Main Street in 1906.

A scenic trolley ride, 1915.

The Ware and Brookfield Street Railway, built in 1906 and discontinued in 1918. The same conductor, Joseph Morin, was on both the first and last runs.

An early touring car with its spare tire securely attached.

Ware ladies on a trip with the family dog.

MAIN STREET, WARE, MASS.   384

Main Street in the 1930s, with the street paved and cars parked in marked slots.

The Hampshire Woolen parking lot in the 1930s. Many employees drove to work by this time.

A long hike. Foot power was the choice of these Ware residents who were setting off on an 8,000-mile hike to San Francisco and back.

Five

Schools and Town Departments

The Fireman's Muster of 1923. The department had been modernized so only one piece of horse-drawn equipment remained in service—the hook and ladder driven by Archie Goyette. The American LaFrance is driven by Dan Hyland while Louis Milos drives the Webb pumper. Louis Berthiume is at the wheel of the Ford on the right. Heavy snows in the winter of this year caused the department to mount equipment on horse-drawn sleighs.

An early horse-drawn pumper on a flat car before the turn of the century.

Ware fire-fighting apparatus in 1884. The fire station doors had not yet been altered to accommodate the larger pieces of equipment.

The current fire station, built in 1939. Ambulance service has been added.

Members of the police department in the late 1920s or early 1930s.

June 20, 1958. Police Chief Stephen Pilch receives the keys to a new Buick from Ernest Gervais as Selectman Roland Gravel looks on.

Ware's first chief of police, Maurice Fitzgerald. He was followed by Chief Bartholomew W. Buckley in 1908.

Reed Municipal Pool. This photograph is thought to have been taken on the pool's opening day, June 14, 1936. The pool was built with Emergency Relief Administration (ERA) labor.

The building used as the town hospital before Mary Lane Hospital was built in the 1920s.

Mary Lane Hospital nearing completion in the latter part of 1923. Much interior work remains to be done.

World War I soldiers. Henry Hevey is second from the left, behind the two men in the front.

The Mt. Carmel School eighth grade graduating class in 1946.

St. Mary's School on South Street, shortly after it was built in 1960. The school was established in 1924 and was originally housed in the lower level of the church.

The old Mt. Carmel School, located off of North Street.

A look at the old South Street School and some of its students in 1880.

The new South Street School after alterations to the building. This building presently houses the Ware Court and the school superintendent's office.

The old High Street School. This building started as a one-story building, with the second story added at a later date. It served as an elementary school, then a high school, and reverted to an elementary school around 1900. It was razed in 1955.

Both the old and new South Street Schools prior to the razing of the older school in 1952.

The high school and junior high school on Church Street in the mid-1920s.

The present high school on West Street, built in 1961.

This may be the oldest print in our collection of Ware schoolchildren, some of whom are without shoes. Perhaps you will find great-grandpa or great-grandma here.

An early photograph of third graders at the old North Street School. The teacher in the impressive hat is thought to be Miss Sibley.

Old North Street School fourth graders. The teacher may be Miss K. Carroll.

Miss Clara Coney's fifth grade class at the High Street School. John T. Storrs and Arthur Eddy are among the children pictured. Recognize anyone else?

The Ware High School Glee Club in 1941. Can you find any familiar faces here?

The senior class of 1946 at the old high school. Many are still young at heart today.

The Ware High School Cadet Corps in 1949. How many can you identify?

Students in Elizabeth Lincoln's high school art class.

Ware High School senior officers, class of 1959.

Senior class Warriors and Maidens of 1951.

The high school play in 1957, with Bob Reznik, Roger Ducharme, Sandra Wilson, and Alan Falk. One of the young ladies remains unidentified.

The Massachusetts Women's Defense Corps, 1946. LaVern Mullens, Florence Lanctot, Theresa Senecal, and Jeannette Couture are pictured.

The Women's Defense Corp encampment at Framingham, Massachusetts, during World War II.

The chimney going up at the new water pumping station on Barnes Street in 1886. It topped off at 80 feet. The pump was steam-driven and fueled by coal until 1916, when the system was converted to electricity.

The street sprinkler. This machine was often used during the summer to keep down the dust which rose from the unpaved streets.

Six

Sports

Ware has long been a sports-oriented town, and an early form of baseball, based on the old New England game of Rounders, was played here before the Civil War. Ware's earliest team, the Washingtons, played with thirteen men on the field, including as many as three "behinds," as they called catchers. Players did not wear gloves and the ball was made of woolen stocking yarn wound on a chunk of rubber covered with leather from shoe uppers stitched in quarters. A runner was out when he was struck by a ball "soaked" or "plugged" at him, which made for a rough game that often ended in a free-for-all. The first side to make twenty-one tallies in even innings was the victor. The Civil War interrupted baseball in this area, but several Ware men joined the Massachusetts 42nd Regiment, Company K, and were able to hone their baseball skills while they guarded bridges in the rear during the Mississippi Campaign. The game was revived after the war, and by around 1912 the Ware baseball team pictured here was outfitted with uniforms, gloves, cleats, and the forerunner of today's baseball caps.

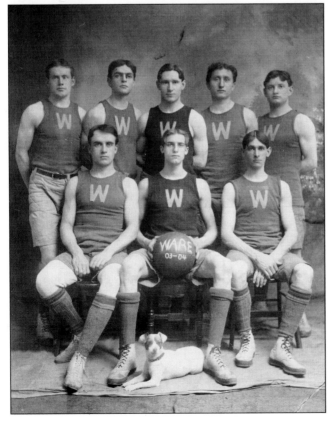

The Ware Athletic Association baseball team in 1922. The manager is Bowler (middle right) and the captain is Flaherty (front right).

The Ware High School basketball team with mascot, 1903–1904.

The Ware High basketball squad, 1939.

The Ware High boys' basketball team with coach and managers, 1947.

The girls' basketball team, 1948.

Ware High School cheerleaders, 1948.

A Ware High football squad, mid-1930s.

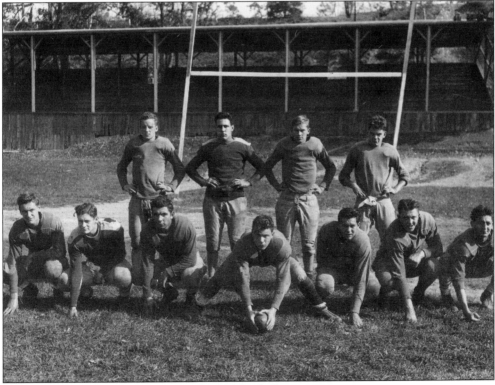

The eleven members of the Ware High 1938 football team.

Football hopefuls; freshmen and beginners in 1958.

Perhaps a game of quoits or horseshoes? Townsmen in suits and hats look toward the camera in this photograph taken around 1890.

Seven
Churches and
Civic Organizations

The Congregational Meeting House, also known as the Ware Center Church. Chartered in 1743, this organization originally built their meetinghouse in 1751, and rebuilt on its present site in 1799. The structure served both as a church and as the seat of town government for the Ware Parish. There is a historic burying ground behind the church which is reserved for ministers and deacons. This photograph shows the old horse sheds at the right rear, and the Ware Center Grange, formerly a school, on the left. The monument visible on the left was erected to the memory of John Read, first proprietor of the town. Although the functional center of town is now to the east, official town notices must still be posted at this old meetinghouse.

TO THE HONOURABLE
JOHN READ
1680 — 1749
PROPRIETOR OF THE MANOUR OF PEACE
BENEFACTOR OF WARE RIVER PARISH
THIS MEMORIAL
IS ERECTED BY THE CITIZENS OF THE TOWN ON THE 150TH
ANNIVERSARY OF ITS INCORPORATION AS A DISTRICT
1911

The 1911 plaque erected by the townspeople in memory of the proprietor of the land forming the major part of Ware.

The Ware Center Grange building, formerly the Ware Center School. Ware Grange No. 164 was established in 1888.

The original East Congregational Church on Church Street, designed by Isaac Damon, before it was destroyed by fire on January 24, 1925, the 98th anniversary of its dedication.

The East Congregational Church, rebuilt after the 1925 fire. The burial grounds are visible on the right.

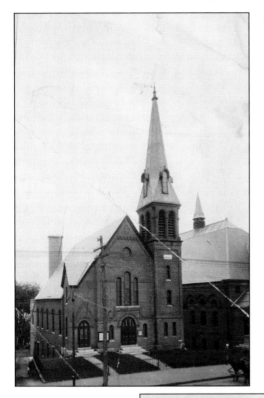

The former Unitarian church on Main Street next to the town hall, originally built in 1846 and burned in 1867. The present building was dedicated in 1869.

The All Saints Church on North Street. Construction was begun in 1888 and the church was dedicated in 1894.

The interior of the All Saints Church.

The original Our Lady of Mt. Carmel Church on Bank Street, erected in 1872 to serve French Canadian Catholics.

The present Mt. Carmel church on Pleasant Street, for which ground was broken in 1923. The architect was Joseph A. Jackson of New Haven and New York.

The old French Congregational church on North Street, also called the Huguenot church.

The Holy Cross Polish National
Catholic Church on Maple Street,
dedicated on July 7, 1929.

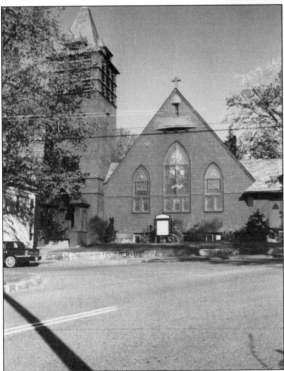

The Trinity Episcopal Church on the
corner of Pleasant and Park Streets.
The cornerstone was laid in October
1888 and the building was dedicated,
debt free, on June 10, 1901.

The old Methodist church, as pictured in 1893 on the occasion of its "Semi-Centennial Jubilee."

New church building. In 1897, this building, with many beautiful stained-glass windows, replaced the old Methodist church. It serves today as the Ware Senior Center.

St. Mary's Church on South Street, erected in 1906. This church was established to serve the Polish population of the town. A "peal" of four bells was hung in 1923, whose first ringing took place on Christmas morning of that year. Different from bells in a "chime," those in a "peal" are all rung together.

The interior of St. Mary's Church.

Father Kolbuch with Frank Jacques, Postmaster St. Onge, and others in the mid-1920s, preparing to mail out the *Postaniec*, the monthly publication of the La Sallette order.

The Sovereign Grace Baptist Church. The Sovereign Grace congregation has met on Palmer Road since September 1973, after the Emanuel Baptist Church stopped meeting on Main Street.

The Kingdom Hall of Jehovah's Witnesses on Gilbertville Road, built by the members over a period of only six months in 1975. Prior to that, the congregation met in West Brookfield.

The former Otis Company counting house, purchased by the Independent Order of Odd Fellows around 1935. They have their meeting rooms on the second floor.

The White Eagle Hall on Pulaski Street, dedicated on November 23, 1930.

A group of Ware Boy Scouts in 1941.

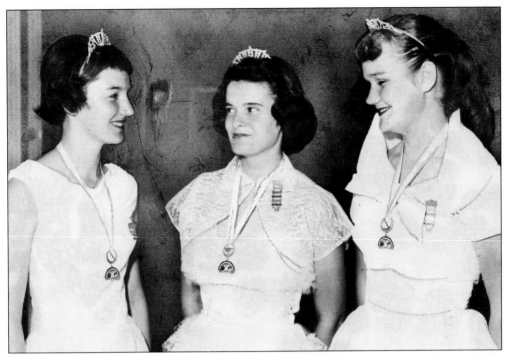

Alice Thatcher, Marjorie Brown, and Margaret Ishom: the Faith, Hope, and Charity of the Rainbow Girls in 1958.

The Ware Men's Club Choir and guests dressed for a concert.

Members of the Ware Explorers' Post 166 at father-son night in 1959. Pictured are John Slattery (president), Alfred Albrecht (advisor), Richard Muisse (speaker), and Richard Mozdzierz (vice president).

Ware Girl Scout cadets on their visit to Washington D.C. in 1968, accompanied by Marie Sorel and others.

The Eden Lodge of Masons home. In 1938 the lodge celebrated its 75th birthday.

The Ware Sons of Veterans in a photograph probably dating from the 1890s.

Prendiville's Military Band in 1883.

The Ware Board of Trade Band. This musical group made its first appearance in 1922 under the direction of Michael Caslis.

Eight
Individuals, Families, and Homes

The Ware Historical Society, founded in June 1962. The first officers are pictured here. They are Floyd Maynard, Ethel Bator, Theresa Aucoin, Pauline Campbell (vice president), Mary Baxter (secretary), and Bill "Mr. Ware" Towlson (president). Due to their vision and hard work, today's historical society has been able to draw on a significant collection of photographs, documents, and artifacts reflecting the history of Ware.

The charter members of the Ware Historical Society in 1962 in the Methodist church.

A Roi (Roy) family group, *c.* 1900, in front of King's Market on East Street near Cherry Street. Minnie Roi was the store proprietor.

An early picture of the Marsh family. Members of this family fought in the American Revolution in 1775.

The Lionel Grise family of Upper Church Street. Pictured here are Francis, Pauline, Mrs. Grise, Marie, Lionel Sr., Lionel Jr., Betty, and Carmel Harris.

A October 6, 1881 photograph of the the D.W. Phelps family's home. Use your magnifying glass to note the various activities represented.

White Eagle officers Joseph Mikuszewski, Frank Koziol, and Ted Gumula in 1959.

A young Mike Houlihan, who ran the Alligator Diner in 1924. As a boy he delivered telegrams. The diner was gutted by fire a few years after it closed.

The organizers of the Ware Industries after the Otis Company left in 1938. Pictured are John H. Schoonmaker, Minot C. Wood, Frank Cebula, Alfred H. Pigeon, Fulton Rindge, B.W. Buckley, and William Deardon.

The Coys Hill building that housed the WARE radio station tower and broadcasting equipment. The studio has been variously located on East Street, Main Street, and South Street, and is now in the Mill Company.

Eleanor Chase, assistant principal of the high school and daughter of Arthur Chase, author of *The History of Ware, Massachusetts*.

Mrs. M. Leroy Greenfield, president of the
Social Science Club from 1941 to 1942. Mr.
Greenfield was superintendent of the Ware
School Department.

Mrs. George D. Storrs, first president of the
Ware Hospital Association and wife of
attorney George Storrs.

Ware's answer to Hollywood, Nancy Howe Hyde, an active actress and producer of many Ware dramatic productions over the years.

Prominent Ware business men of the 1930s and 1940s. Pictured are Bernie Satz, Leonard Campbell, Bill Deardon, and Don Howe.

The wedding of Clarissa Como and Leo Durand. The Durands have long been prominent in the Ware business community, running a successful store on Main Street for several generations.

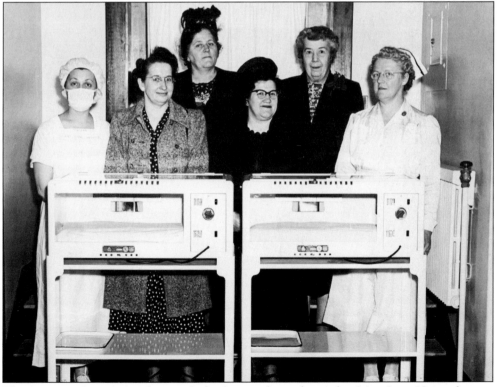

The American Legion Auxiliary with the first incubator donated to Mary Lane Hospital.

"The Castle," built on Castle Street in 1862.

The Seidel House in Ware Center, originally the Center Church parsonage.

Nine
Celebrations and Events

A postcard of the "Ware alligator." In June 1922 Ware achieved a measure of national publicity, or if you prefer, notoriety, when a 5-foot alligator was reported in "Dismal Swamp" on Gilbertville Road and later in the Ware River. The story was picked up by national news services and people came from far and near to catch a glimpse of this creature. The local paper offered a $50 reward for its capture, and enterprising youngsters sold peanuts and popcorn at the scene. The animal never was caught, but it gave rise to "The Alligator Diner;" "The Ware Alligators," a semi-professional baseball team; and *The Ware Alligator*, a high school student magazine.

A wagon of children in a parade before 1900. Note that the town hall doesn't yet have its clock.

Mounted marshals for Ware's 150th anniversary celebration in 1911, led by Chief Marshall John H. Neff.

A 1913 photograph of the all-female cast from one of the Social Science Club plays, taken in Mrs. Gilbert's garden.

An old-fashioned minstrel show, presented in the town hall. The producer is not identified, but it is believed to be a local organization.

Ste. Cecile Conciel #115's float in an early parade. Included are Eva Charpentier, Martha Petit, and Roland Jacques.

A parade float of the Liberty Lodge Independent Companions of America. This organization is listed in John and Dorothy Conkey's *History of Ware, Massachusetts 1911–1960* as being one of the Ware organizations that existed in the second decade of the twentieth century.

An interesting Ware Grange float from somewhere in the 1920s.

Part of the 150th anniversary parade on Main Street in 1911.

Another 1911 photograph. The town's fire equipment is all trimmed up for the parade.

The Army-Navy E Award, given to Ware Coupling and Nipple Company during World War II. Don Howe and John Schoonmaker are pictured with service personnel.

The Army-Navy Production Award, won by the Ware and Hampshire Mills in August 1942. George Morgan, Earl McCann, David Carroll, and Ludovic Gariepy were at the flag-raising ceremony. Lloyd Merrill is at the organ.

The E-Awards ceremony. Judge John H. Schoonmaker is shown here welcoming employees, guests, and Army-Navy personnel.

The World War II "welcome home" celebration on Flag Day 1947. About 500 veterans marched in this event, and they were later joined by 300 more for a clambake in Grenville Park, followed by a dance in the evening to finish out the day.

Two Ware World War I vets, "Cy" Morin and "Al" Sorel, at the "welcome home" celebration.

Ware veterans and the high school band at the Memorial Day parade ceremony in front of the town hall in 1947.

Girl Scouts marching to the Mt. Carmel and Aspen Grove cemeteries on Memorial Day, 1947.

World War I veteran Emile St. Onge on North Street, Memorial Day, 1947.

Bicentennial Queen Elaine Wood with her attendants, Ursule Gumula (left) and Kathy Lussier (right).

The Ware Town Seal float in the bicentennial parade. Donald Riggie is the Indian.

A rather large—yet old-fashioned—dinner. More than 3,400 people attended this supper, which filled the Main Street from North Street to Nenameseck Square. The menu consisted of good old beans and brown bread.

Students and a snow sculpture at Ware High School's first winter carnival.

The Ware High School art class during the United States bicentennial celebration.

Ten

Disasters

Looking toward Nenameseck Square from the south side of the Ware River on South Street after the flood and hurricane of September 1938. The South Street bridge has been swept away, along with sections of the street. The photograph was taken shortly before the collapse of the fire station, which is shown here leaning precipitously to one side. Homes and buildings along the river edge show various levels of destruction. During the height of the flood, the south side of town was cut off from the rest of Ware and communication with the outside world was by ham radio only.

The East Congregational Church fire on the night of January 24, 1925.

The aftermath of the January 1944 fire which started in the Grise Bag Company and destroyed six small businesses. The damage estimate from this disasterous blaze was one million dollars.

Looking up South Street over the bridge from the Nenameseck Square area during the 1938 flood. A corner of the fire station can be seen at the lower right. Note the crowd gathered across the river.

A temporary bridge across the Ware River in 1938, used to reconnect the south and north sides of the town.

The collapsed fire station tower in September 1938.

"Woolenville Town Hall," set up as the administration center for the south side of town when it was cut off by flood waters in 1938.

A family trying to cope with the 1938 hurricane and its watery aftermath.

Hurricane damage on Church Street. This is the McLaurin house in 1938.

The Mary Lane Hospital after the hurricane.

A flooded West Street. Note the truck with only the top visible.

The site of the present Phillip Plaza during the 1938 flood.

Rebuilding the dam on the Ware River above the South Street bridge.

Pulaski Street (formerly Water Street) after the flood waters receded.

A combination of flood and hurricane damage in 1938.

Damage from an earlier storm. In 1906 a small tornado swept through a Ware cemetery.

The Storrs Block burns, scarring Main Street. The Friendly Restaurant occupies the site today.

Acknowledgments

As Ware Historical Society members working under the direction of Curator Lynne Bassett on a project to organize and classify the society's collection of historic material, we found the photographs in that collection connected us in a visual and charming way to the town of Ware—both as it was and to its evolution into what it is today. The idea of a book was born of our wish to share these unique images with our friends and neighbors. The authors, with the assistance of Marguerite Seidel, Jeanne Phaneuf, and Elizabeth Lincoln, all members of the Ware Historical Society, then began the challenging and time-consuming task of selecting over two hundred photographs for inclusion in this book. In order to assemble as much material as possible from which to make our selections, we appealed to the community for the donation or loan of historic photographs in private collections. The response was more than we could have hoped for, and we extend our heart-felt gratitude to the following for the donation or loan of photographs or other assistance:

Barbara Bullock, Madeleine Cebula, Les Campbell, Mary Ann DeSantis, Lenny Demers, Philip W. Dick, Rose Duval, Robert Hevey, Nancy Hyde, Justine Jacques, Jean Ligawiec, Roger and Elizabeth Lincoln, Jeanne Lund, Rachel Mace, Arline McBride, John McQuaid, Jeannette Mondor, Jeanne Phaneuf, Sam Rindge, Marie Sorel, Stasia Towlson, Charlotte Tyler, Bernard Wilson, Lyndon Wilson, and Senior Center Members.

Our sincere thanks go to all who have discussed our project with us and supported our efforts.